Pebble® Plus

Construction Zone

Building a House

by JoAnn Early Macken

Consulting Editor: Gail Saunders-Smith, PhD

Consultant: Chris Dauk, owner
Dauk Construction Inc.
Eagle Lake, Minnesota

Capstone
press®

Mankato, Minnesota

Pebble Plus is published by Capstone Press,
151 Good Counsel Drive, P.O. Box 669, Mankato, Minnesota 56002.
www.capstonepress.com

1 2 3 4 5 6 14 13 12 11 10 09

Library of Congress Cataloging-in-Publication Data
Macken, JoAnn Early, 1953–
    Building a house / By JoAnn Early Macken.
    p. cm. — (Pebble plus — Construction zone)
    Includes bibliographical references and index.
    Summary: "Simple text and photographs present the construction of a house, including information on the workers
and equipment needed" — Provided by publisher.
    ISBN-13: 978-1-4296-2258-5 (hardcover)
    ISBN-10: 1-4296-2258-X (hardcover)
    1. House construction — Juvenile literature. I. Title.
TH4811.5.M35 2009
690'.837 — dc22   2008027657

Editorial Credits
Megan Peterson, editor; Ted Williams, designer; Jo Miller, photo researcher

Photo Credits
Capstone Press/Karon Dubke, 21
fotolia/Greg Pickens, cover; meaille.luc@wanadoo.fr, 11
Getty Images Inc./Stone/Lester Lefkowitz, 7
iStockphoto/George Peters, 19; Terry J Alcorn, 13
Shutterstock/Christina Richards, 9; Jim Parkin, 1; Lisa F. Young, 15, 17; Stephen Coburn, 5

Note to Parents and Teachers

The Construction Zone set supports national science standards related to science and
technology. This book describes and illustrates house construction. The images support early
readers in understanding the text. The repetition of words and phrases helps early readers learn
new words. This book also introduces early readers to subject-specific vocabulary words, which
are defined in the Glossary section. Early readers may need assistance to read some words and
to use the Table of Contents, Glossary, Read More, Internet Sites, and Index sections of
the book.

Table of Contents

Planning

A family needs a new house.

An architect draws a plan.

Construction Begins

A bulldozer clears the site.

A backhoe digs a hole

for the basement.

backhoe

A cement truck pours concrete.

It makes a strong foundation.

The framing crew builds

the floors, walls, and roof.

They hang the doors

and windows.

Roofers nail shingles

on the roof.

Vinyl siding is added

to the outside of the house.

Inside Work

Electricians put in wires, lights, and outlets.

Plumbers put in water pipes.

They add toilets, bathtubs,

and sinks.

Workers put insulation

in the walls.

They hang drywall over it.

Then they get the walls ready

for painting.

Moving In

The house is finished.

The family is ready to move in.

Glossary

architect — a person who designs and draws plans for buildings, bridges, and other construction projects

backhoe — a digging machine with a bucket at the end of a long arm

bulldozer — a powerful tractor with a wide blade at the front; bulldozers move earth, rocks, and rubble.

concrete — a mixture of cement, water, sand, and gravel that hardens when it dries

drywall — a large sheet of inside finishing material; drywall is also called Sheetrock.

insulation — a material that stops heat or cold from entering or leaving a building

shingle — a flat, thin piece of wood or other material used to cover roofs

vinyl — a type of siding made of plastic

Read More

Macken, JoAnn Early. *Construction Crews.* Construction Zone. Mankato, Minn.: Capstone Press, 2008.

Nelson, Robin. *From Tree to House.* Start to Finish. Minneapolis: Lerner, 2004.

Pallotta, Jerry. *The Construction Alphabet Book.* Watertown, Mass.: Charlesbridge, 2006.

Internet Sites

FactHound offers a safe, fun way to find educator-approved Internet sites related to this book.

Here's what you do:
1. Visit *www.facthound.com*
2. Choose your grade level.
3. Begin your search.

This book's ID number is 9781429622585.

FactHound will fetch the best sites for you!

Index

Word Count: 113

Grade: 1

Early-Intervention Level: 22

24